Anne S

MW00655316

101 THOUGHTS to make you THINK.

Illustrations by: Ronnie Bates

By Anne Sadovsky and Elexis Rice:
101 Thoughts For Becoming the Real You

Copyright ©1988 by Anne Sadovsky

All rights reserved.

No part of this book may be reproduced in any form without written permission from the publisher.

Published by Taylor Publishing Company
1550 West Mockingbird Lane
Dallas, Texas 75235

Illustrations by Ronnie Bates

Library of Congress Cataloging-in-Publication Data

Sadovsky, Anne
Anne Sadovsky's 101 thoughts to make you think/ illustrations by Ronnie Bates.
p. cm.
ISBN 0-87833-735-0: $5.95
I. Title. II. Title: 101 thoughts to make you think. III. Title: Anne Sadovsky's one hundred one thoughts to make you think. IV. Title: Anne Sadvosky's one hundred and one thoughts to make you think.
PN6331.S23 1991
818′.5402—dc20 90-21573
CIP

Printed in the United States of America

10 9 8 7 6 5 4 3 2 1

Words of wisdom come to us from many sources; our mothers, our grandfathers, the newspapers and television. Sometimes we hear them from our minister, we read them in a book or we hear a speaker say something that really hits home. There's an old saying that goes *"When the student is ready the teacher appears."*

I want to say thank you to the whole universe and every human being whose path has crossed mine. They *all* get credit for the things I've learned and am about to share with you.

You will find messages you've heard, read or thought, maybe worded differently, and you will understand that we all drink from the same cup of common knowledge.

Therefore, you shouldn't be surprised when others know what you know.

Anne Sadovsky

We all drink from the same cup of common knowledge. Don't be surprised when others know what you know.

1

Two of life's greatest lessons: If it ain't broke, don't fix it.

2

But if it's broke,
and you can't fix it,
accept it and don't
grieve your heart
out over it.

Talk less
and listen more.
That's why we have
more ears than
mouths.

3

Life is a many splendored thing. Count your blessings.

4

Life is what you
make it.
Make sunshine!

5

Don't judge a book by its cover. Some great new friends come in plain wrappers.

6

7

Practice does make perfect. Remember the first time you tried to parallel park?

How do you stay happy about life? Think of the alternative!

8

Enthusiasm is the spice of life. You get it by getting sold on living.

9

In all of life there are choices. Choose the best you.

10

11

Care about your world. Today's society says we're using our resources. Tomorrow's society may say we stole them.

12

Success isn't
measured in dollars,
it's measured in
joy…and peace
…and love
…and sharing.

What you earn is directly related to what you learn.

13

The opposite of regrets is risk. Take a few and you won't have so many regrets.

Greet warmly.
Your face should
say "Welcome,
I'm glad you're here."

15

Don't talk about yourself first. Find out about others.

16

17

People who get what they want —*ask!*

18

We all have to show and tell. Make it colorful and interesting and others will listen.

19

When you work
because you love it
and not for money,
money comes more
abundantly.

20

Happy customers talk, unhappy customers talk louder.

Keep in touch. Being unforgettable pays off.

21

Market yourself, market your product, serve your customers.

22

Guaranteed success!

(It worked for Lee Iacocca.)

Part of real
success is doing
something you love
every day so well
that you get
paid for it!

24

A *"to do"* list works. You get organized and as you mark things off, you see your accomplishments.

25

You get paid from the customer's money. Always remember that.

Spoiled customers are yours forever.

26

27

Customers are tired of paying for rudeness because they get so much of it free. Never be rude to your customer.

Life is a degree in psychology.

28

Receive compliments with *"Thanks, I'm glad you noticed."*

29

The only person
you can change
is you.
So love and accept
others as they are.

Your childhood
is over.
It's time to stop
blaming your
parents and get on
with your life.

31

Here's what I've learned the hard way. People march to the beat of a different drummer and that's OK.

Eye contact in communication shows that you're tuned in, or turned off.

33

Childhood conditioning has power. Are you still cleaning your plate so the children in China won't starve?

34

35

You are in charge
of you.
That gives you
total control.

36

Your mind controls
your brain.
Your brain controls
your body, so you
can lose weight
or stop smoking.
Just make up
your mind.

Time is life,
waste not one
precious moment.
Use part of it to
smell the roses.

37

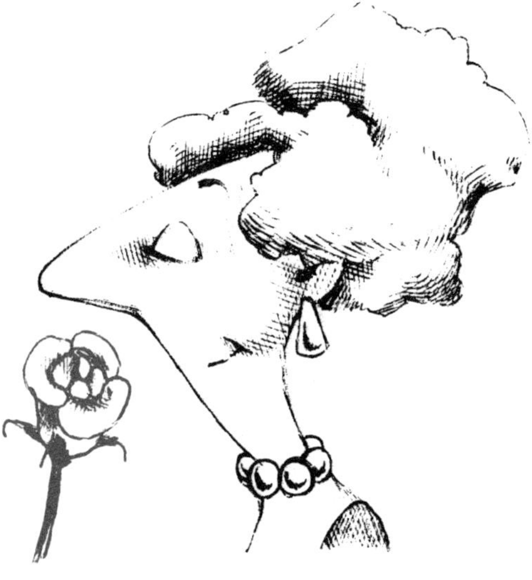

The speed of the leader is the speed of the gang. Be a good leader.

38

39

One of God's greatest jokes is giving us children who don't think and believe the way we do.

And some of our greatest lessons are the ones we learn from rearing those children.

Develop charisma.
Smile more,
make new friends,
don't argue and
mirror the positive
emotions of others.

40

41

What you say to
your children when
they're little has
a lot to do with
what they are when
they're big.
Say nice things.

42

When you touch someone else, a charge of your energy goes through them. Give more hugs.

If life were all
easy and fun,
how would we learn
anything new?

43

44

Your mind is a computer. Garbage in, garbage out.

Repeat to yourself
over and over
every day:
I am a unique
and wonderful
person.

Write it down and tape it to the mirror. Read it while you brush your teeth!

The only person you can change is you.

46

Visualization
is powerful.
See yourself happy
and successful.

47

The only way you can change your life is to change what you think.

48

Act happy,
act confident,
act like a winner.
Practice makes
perfect!

Every day of life
is for lessons.
What have you
learned today?

50

Focus on what you are, not what you aren't.

51

You truly are
what you think
and believe.
Think and believe
only the best.

52

You have to start today what you'd like to accomplish tomorrow.

53

54

Open your mind. There is no more proof that you haven't lived before than there is that you have.

55

Only when you
love yourself
can others love you!

56

The determining factor of your behavior and success is how you feel about you.

All that matters
in life is how
you react to what
happens to you.

57

Plan what you want,
write it down,
think about it a
lot, and then
enjoy it.
It will be yours.

Shin kicking doesn't motivate. Praise does.

59

Lots of people
are lonely.
Say hello and *smile!*

60

Think the best.
Accept only the best.
Enjoy the best.

61

Don't say,
I'll try."
Say, "*I will."*

Decide what you want out of life. Write it down.

Read it four times a day. Don't tell everyone. Too many will tell you that you can't.

63

Enthusiasm is the energy that puts pep in your step and a song in your soul.

64

Tenacity is knocking again on the door that slammed in your face.

65

Criticism is more destructive than constructive.

66

Give more time toward improving others than criticizing them.

67

Do the same for yourself.

Look for the sunny side of every rainy day.

68

When you believe
in you,
others will,
too.

People forgive a lot of things, but they never forget unfair treatment.

70

Nothing to do makes life drag by.

71

Being busy has
its trade-off.
It makes your life
go a lot faster.

72

You can stop
wishing for more
time.
You have all
there is.

If you could choose between happiness and misery, which would you choose? You can choose!

74

Broaden your scope by trying something new.

75

Today is the first day of the rest of your life. What are you doing right now?

76

Flowers blossom
toward the
sunshine.
Are you the sunshine
for the people
in your life?

78

Start your day by reading something positive, save the front page for later.

Have balance in your life. Strive for the right amount of work and play and rest.

79

If you really want the apple, you have to go out on a limb.

80

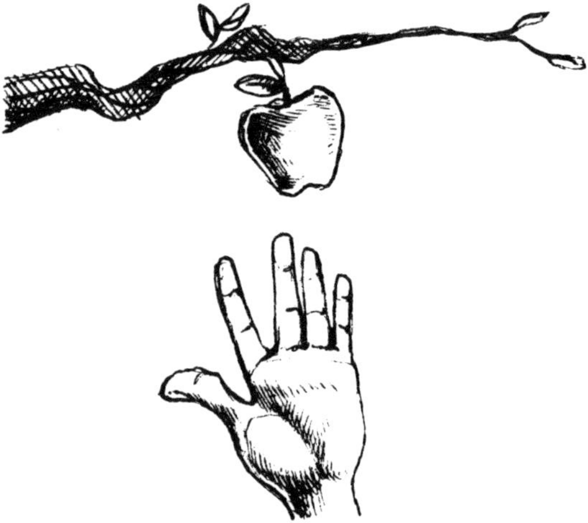

Do you know what you want to be when you grow up? And how to get there?

81

Flexibility gives you possibility you've never thought of.

82

Believe yourself when you say *"I can."*

83

Who told you that you couldn't?

84

And why did you believe them?

Here's my only guarantee: Life is going to keep changing.

85

86

When you say,
"But I've always done it this way,"
you're a stumbling block, who gets left behind.

Having the ability to hang in there allows you to take advantage of more opportunities than those who quit.

87

Fear of failure makes you fail. Be brave enough to win!

88

It does matter
how you look.
Do the best with
what you've got
every day.

89

Growing older is grand. Along with the wrinkles you get experience and wisdom.

90

91

How your friends and families remember you after you're gone is your responsibility today.

92

Never stop learning and growing.
It keeps the mind working longer than the knees.

Who's going to take care of you when you're old? Plan to do it yourself! You could beat it by staying young.

93

We come into the world crying, no teeth and drooling. Take care of yourself so you don't go out the same way.

94

95

Unconditional love is when someone loves you in spite of you.

96

Do you know where
you really want to
be right now?
Close your eyes.
Now open them
and look around.
You <u>are</u> where you
want to be
right now.

97

Time really does heal all wounds. Don't give up; just give it more time.

Things really do turn out for the best.

Remember that when things seem all wrong.

98

Forgive yourself and others...then get on with living.

99

Once in a while
check on yourself.
Ask your family
"How am I doing?"

100

101

Real sin is deliberately hurting another human being.

About the Author:

A Texas native, Anne Sadovsky is a popular speaker and widely published author on motivational and educational subjects. She is a frequent guest on radio and television talk shows and has appeared on *Hour Magazine.* Her success story has been written about in many newspapers and magazines including *Money* and *Ladies Home Journal*. She has served on the governing boards of many trade groups and professional organizations. An honorary of Pi Sigma Epsilon marketing fraternity, Anne Sadovsky is listed in *Who's Who of American Women* and *Notable Women of Texas.* She has been awarded a Certified Speaking Professional designation by the National Speakers Association — a designation held by fewer than 150 people.